THE
MILLENNIUM
GENERATION

THE
MILLENNIUM
GENERATION

PHOTOGRAPHS BY ROBIN LAURANCE

INTRODUCED BY SIR PETER USTINOV

British Library Cataloguing-in-Publication Data

A catalogue record for this book is available from the British Library

ISBN 0-500-281521

Printed and bound in Hong Kong by Everbest

CONTENTS

NAZik

SOUTH AFRICA

SOUTH AFRICA

AUSTRALIA

LUXEMBOURG

PAKISTAN

ENGLAND

SPAIN

ENGLAND

MALAYSIA

CHINA

JAPAN

USA

FOREWORD

Anniversaries are a time to celebrate. This book is intended to be a celebration both of the start of the new millennium and those who will shape its early years – the young people whose lives, in a bewildering and sometimes riotous mix, will come to fruition as it starts, and whose decisions and character will mould it.

Robin Laurance's brief was to capture the anticipation of this moment and to produce a portrait of the hopes and ambitions of what we have called 'The Millennium Generation'. Much of the book is about preparation – about the important rituals, the 'Rites of Passage' – and about the sheer hard work and dedication which young people put in to ready themselves for what lies ahead – whether it's our sequence of the novice Buddhist monk in Japan, a dancer from the Royal Ballet School in London or Masai children learning to look after their flocks.

Another theme is the commonality of the challenges and concerns shared by young people of different cultures. Robin's collection of portraits of school leaders thousands of miles distant from each other emphasizes this, while his images of two schools in Southern Africa points up the contrasts in resources which can obtain across only a few kilometres.

This book sets out to celebrate the energy and determination of the new generation. But there are inevitable reminders here, which need no words, of the harsher side, of the poverty and deprivation which is the lot of so many. They remain, however, within a context – the context of hope and of celebration: part of a tapestry which Robin Laurance has woven for us of the face of the Millennium Generation as it prepares for life after the year 2000.

Finally, a word about ICI and why we sponsored this project. ICI is one of the world's leading specialty products and paint companies. Whether it is the adhesive which holds your sports shoes together, the paint on your wall, the flavouring of your yoghurt, or even the distinctive fragrance in your perfume, the chances are that somewhere, somehow, ICI touched your life today. With locations in over 50 countries, and over 40,000 people working directly for us worldwide, we have a keen interest in how the Millennium Generation will behave and how we can continue to satisfy their needs. But our staff are concerned in other ways, too. From the start of its 73-year history, ICI has believed in contributing to the communities where its operations are based. So throughout this book you will find projects assisted by ICI, whether it is an intensive care unit in a Rotterdam hospital, a group of schoolboys transfixed by an experiment brought by an ICI-supported science caravan in the north-east of England, pupils in schools built and financed over many years near our plants in India and Pakistan, or the support provided by a new member of the ICI family – National Starch – to education about teenage pregnancy in the United States.

Now, please join us in celebrating the Millennium Generation.

MARTIN ADENEY

INTRODUCTION

I have always thought that still photographs are more eloquent and more evocative than many feet of moving picture. A moment in time, indelibly frozen, challenges the imagination of the onlooker, whereas a moving picture does much of the work otherwise left to the imagination. As if to prove my point, here are these exquisite pictures captured by Robin Laurance in many parts of the world, in which babies, children and adolescents of many colours and traditions are linked by their profound attachment to the human race. Even an ardent believer in a military solution to all our problems will be softened by these photographs to a point of admitting that even if one side in a conflict is more guilty than another, war itself is the most criminal of all activities, with its addiction to the indiscriminate in its striving for results. And now, along comes the millennium to make us conscious of the dizzy speed of technical progress in this day and age, and yet the dreaming infants in this collection are the same basic human material as that of the sleeping Christchild in Early Renaissance pictures from Italy or the chubby cherubs from the High Baroque. What kind of life awaits them? And how will they learn to cope with the sort of existence unknown even to their parents? Where once the brightest source of light apart from the sun was the candle, and the most rapid form of transport the galloping horse, now speed has to be translated into understandable form by computers, while psychedelic light effects, which would have sent people mad five centuries ago, are now the staple form of illumination in any self-respecting discotheque. The strain on human sensibilities has never been as intense, nor has the norm been further from the instinctive reaction to things. These children will awaken to a life in which all control is remote and distances are accurate to within a millionth of a centimetre. And once all knowledge is immediately accessible, of what use will art be, of what use literature or music? In a world deaf to doubt and free choice – a world without question marks – what is there left but a full stop? Poor children, keeping the planet on an even keel will be even more difficult than ever before! And yet there are saving graces. The old, the traditional, still holds a few winning cards in its hands. Seeing the child in its swaddling clothes put me in mind of the fact that among those babies bereft of all movement by this draconian Biblical restraint, not a single case of cot-death has been reported. Wisdom is ageless. That too is expressed in these wonderful pictures.

SIR PETER USTINOV
1999

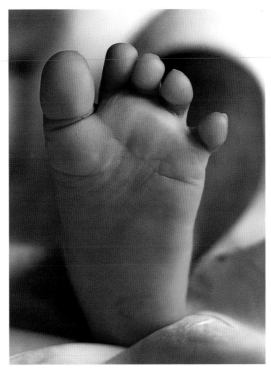

Opposite: ENGLAND, above: SOUTH AFRICA

A journey of a thousand miles must begin with a single step

CHINESE PROVERB

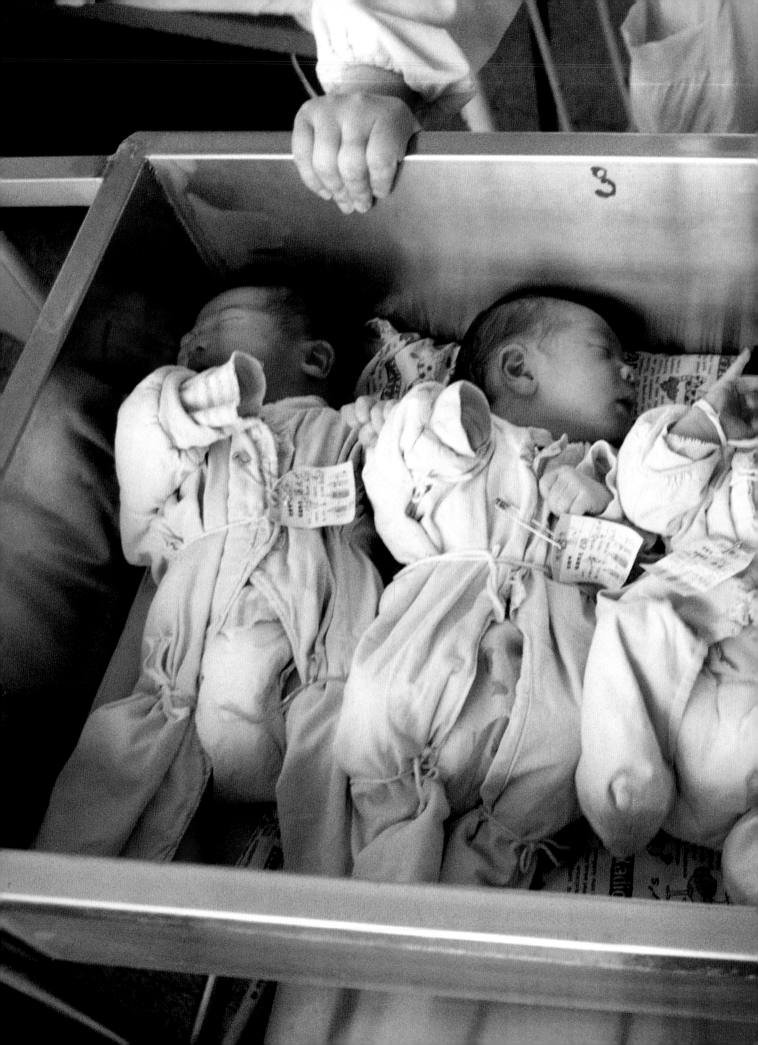

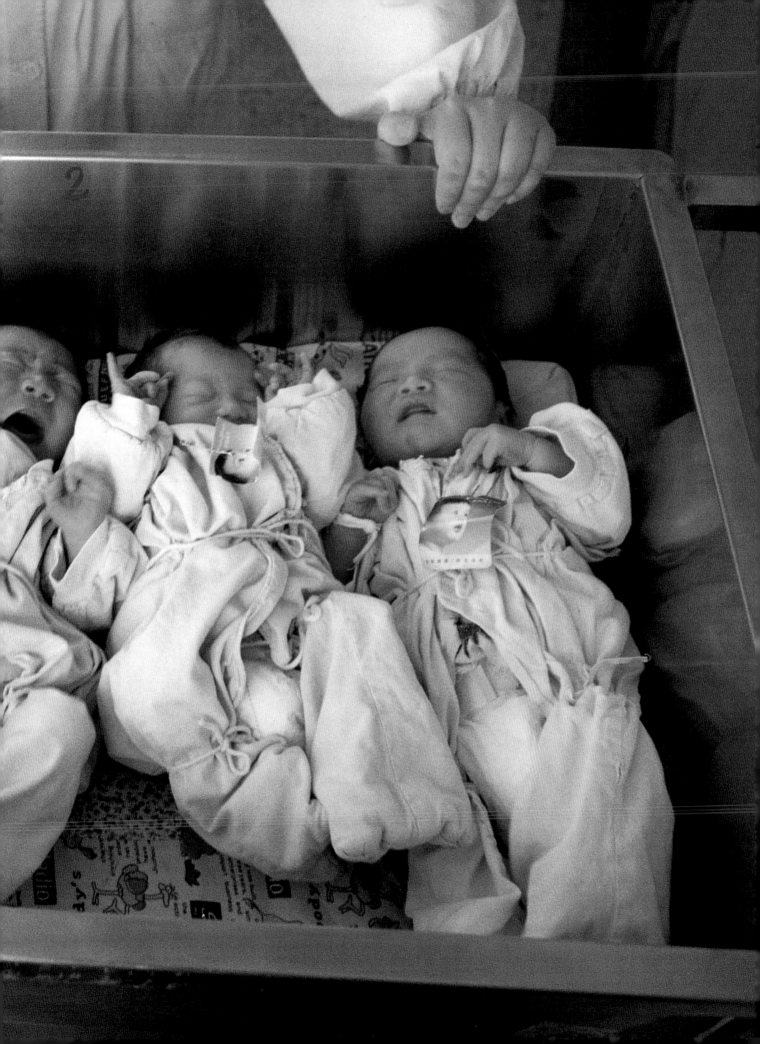

Above and preceding pages: CHINA

Above CHINA, opposite: HOLLAND

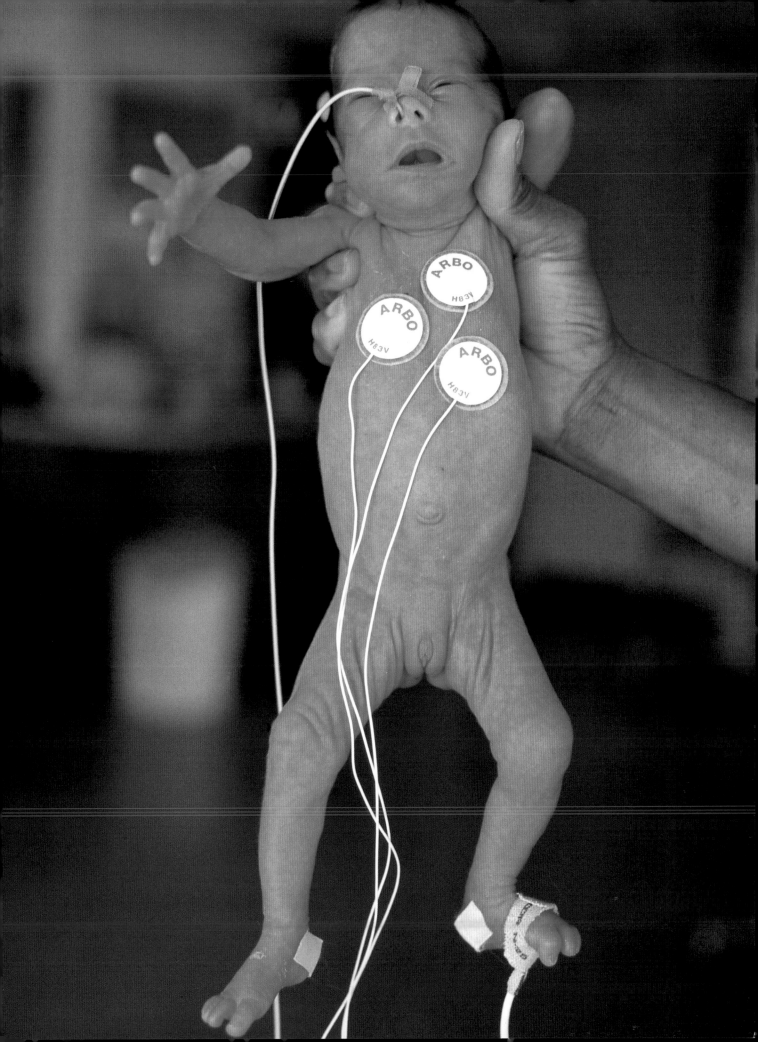

MOROCCO

SOUTH AFRICA

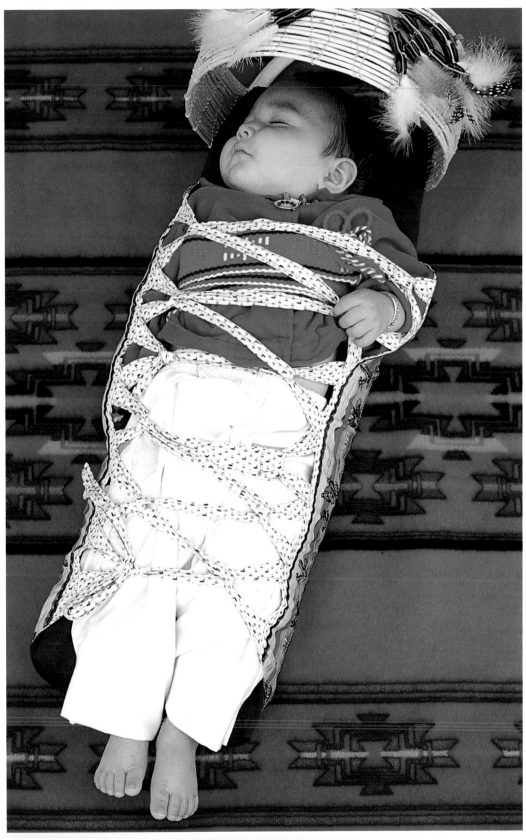

Above: USA, overleaf: SOUTH AFRICA

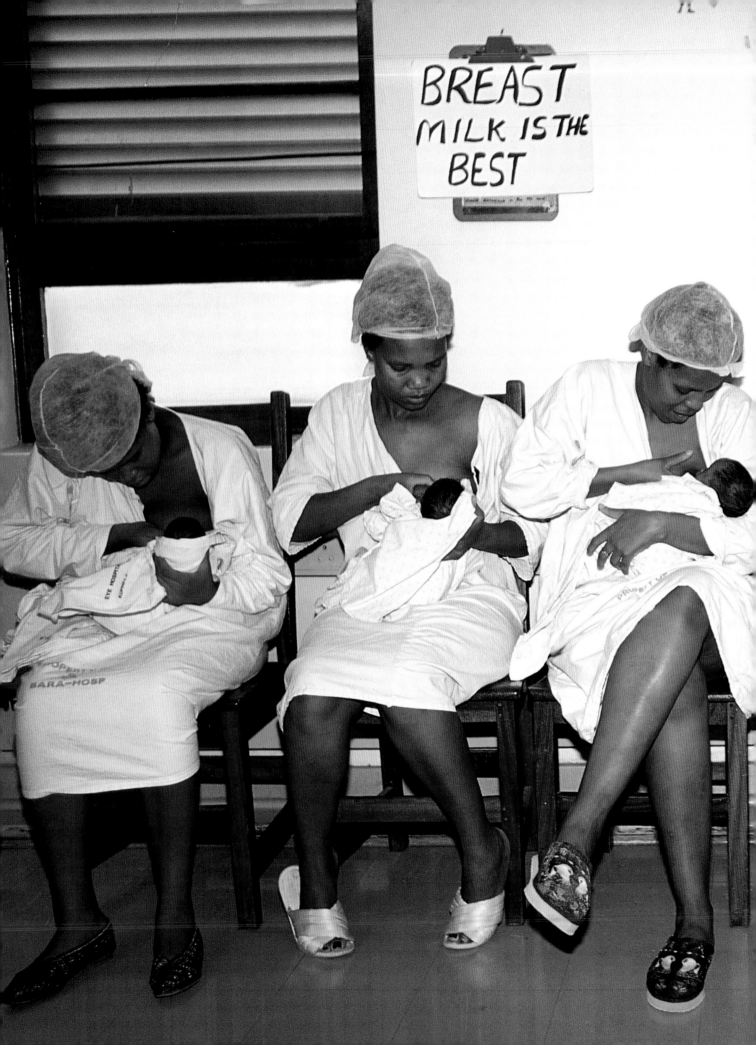

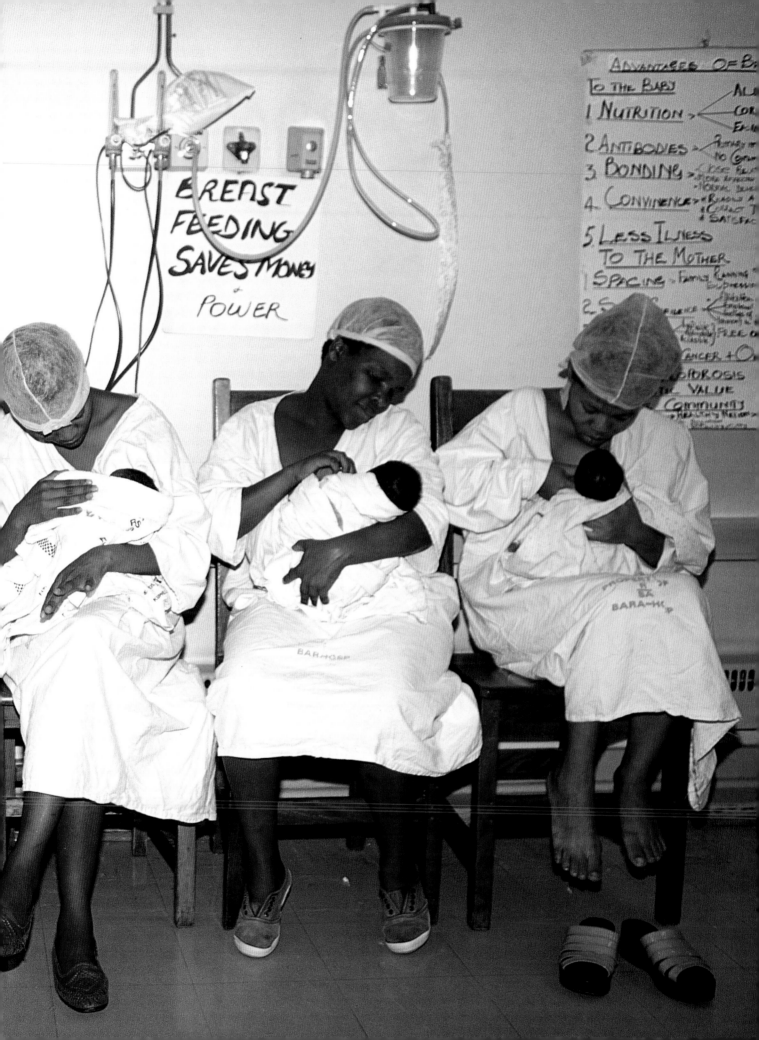

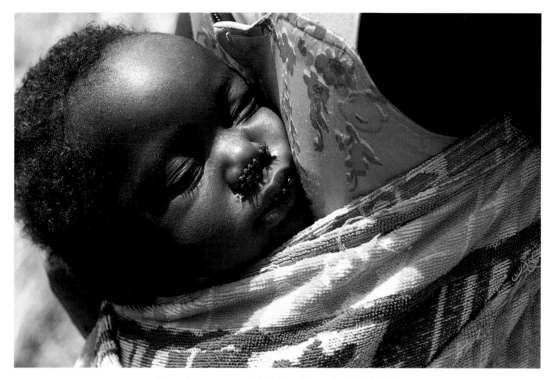

Preceding pages: OMAN, above: ZIMBABWE

Above, Zimbabwe: a village clinic.

Page 12, Oxford, England: taking sibling soundings.

Page 13, Soweto, South Africa: Chris Hani Baragwanath Hospital.

Pages 14-16, Shanghai, China: Changning Woman and Infant Hospital.
ICI is supporting the new Hope hospital in Shanghai.

Page 17, Rotterdam, Holland:
Intensive Therapy Unit, Sophia Children's Hospital, which receives
support from ICI.

Page 18, top, the Mid-Atlas mountains, Morocco.
Bottom, Umtata, Transkei, South Africa.

Page 19, Arizona, USA: Navajo powwow at Window Rock.

Pages 20-21, Soweto, South Africa: the premature baby unit at
the Chris Hani Baragwanath Hospital.

Pages 22-23, Oman: desert Bedouin.

JAPAN

*Nature without learning is
blind, learning apart from nature
is fractional, and practice in the
absence of both is aimless*

PLUTARCH, c. AD 100

Preceding pages: MALDIVES, above: PAKISTAN

Above: PERU, opposite: INDONESIA

Preceding pages: INDONESIA, above: SOUTH AFRICA

Above and opposite: SOUTH AFRICA

Preceding pages: AUSTRALIA, above: INDIA

JORDAN

PAKISTAN

ENGLAND

ENGLAND

PAKISTAN

INDONESIA

Above: USA, opposite TURKEY

HOLLAND

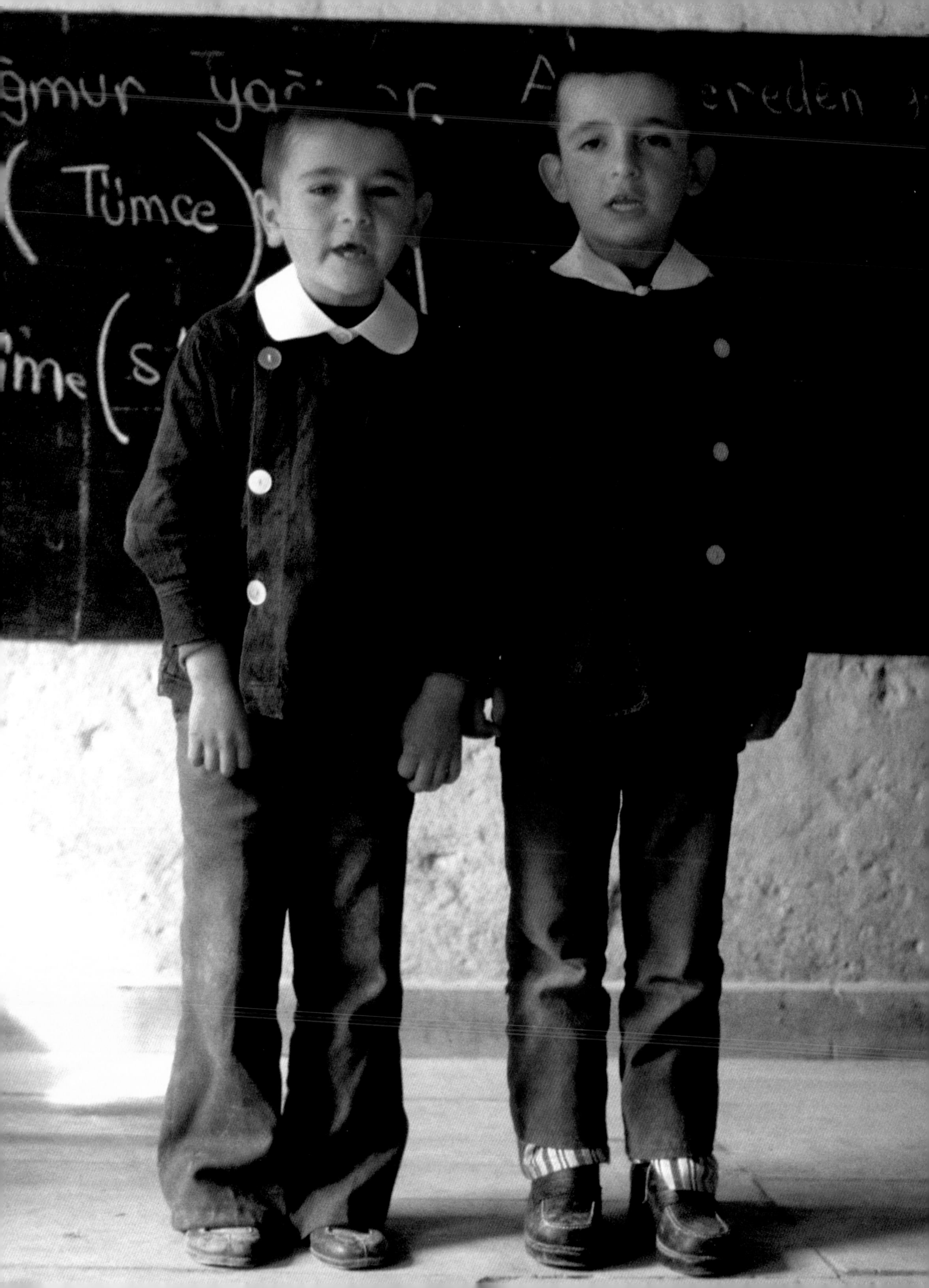
Tümce

BRAZIL

Above, Rondonia, Brazil: the school 'bus' collects children from a tin mine.

Page 25, Tokyo, Japan: boys of the Gakushuin school.

Pages 26-27, Himmafushi Island, The Maldives: returning to the classroom.

Page 28, top, Lahore, Pakistan: the schoolrun.
Bottom, Lake Titicaca, Peru:
children on the floating islands leave for school on the mainland at Puno.

Pages 29-31, Sumatra, Indonesia:
homebound by 'taxi' near Medan and by foot in the northern province of Aceh.

Page 32, top, Pietermaritzburg, South Africa: Hilton College.
Bottom, Katlehong township, South Africa: Monde primary school.

Page 33, Pietermaritzburg, South Africa: St Anne's College.

Pages 34-35, New South Wales, Australia: North Star primary school.

Page 36, top, Calcutta, India: classes for the city's slum children are run by
senior girls at Loreto House School.
Bottom, Dan, southern Jordan: the village school.

Page 37, Lahore, Pakistan: prefects at Aitchison College.

Page 38, top, High Wycombe, England:
pre-prep pupils at Godstowe Preparatory School.
Bottom, Teesside, England: young researchers in the ICI science caravan.

Page 39, top, Karachi, Pakistan: the ABSA school for the deaf,
a project supported by ICI Pakistan.
Bottom, Bali, Indonesia: junior school at Ubud.

Page 40, top, Parksville, USA: Gan Israel summer camp.
Bottom, Rozenburg, Holland: the Educational Farm project,
a project supported by ICI.

Page 41, Central Anatolia, Turkey: a village school.

AUSTRALIA

When work is a pleasure,
life is a joy! When work is a duty,
life is slavery

MAXIM GORKY, *THE LOWER DEPTHS,* 1903

Opposite: PAKISTAN, above: AUSTRALIA

Above: IRELAND, overleaf: INDIA

45

Opposite: PERU, above: INDIA

TANZANIA

ENGLAND

PAKISTAN

IRAN

Above, Isfahan, Iran: carpet worker.

Page 43, New South Wales, Australia: working the family farm.

Page 44, Lahore, Pakistan: workers start young in the automotive workshops.

Page 45, top, Queensland, Australia: hunting wild pigs can be a profitable
occupation for teenagers in Goondiwindi.
Bottom, Dublin, Ireland: tea break on the rounds.

Page 46-47, Varanasi, India: already a veteran of her trade at 12 years old,
Rita waits to sell flowers to Hindu pilgrims.

Page 48, Tambomachay, Peru: young shepherds tend their llamas and alpacas.

Page 49, top, Rajasthan, India: fetching water is the work of young girls.
Bottom, northern Tanzania: caring for and milking the calves and young goats is
the work of the junior female members of a Masai family.

Page 50, Sussex, England:
weekend worker on the Kent and East Sussex Railway.

Page 51, Lahore, Pakistan: motor mechanic.

USA

*Oh, what a power is motherhood,
possessing a potent spell.
All women alike fight fiercely
for a child*

EURIPIDES, *ORESTES*, c. 405 BC

USA

USA

USA

Above and pages 53-59, Florida, USA:
if your child has above-average looks, he or she could be a
money-spinner. Tempted by generous prize money, mothers parade their
offspring at beauty pageants throughout America's Southern states.
In these pictures the children, none of them more than nine years old, compete
for the top prize of US $10,000 in the Continental Miss and Master Finals
at Altamonte Springs.

Above: BELGIUM, overleaf: TANZANIA

*F*or when the One Great Scorer
comes to mark against your name,
He writes – not that you won
or lost – but how you played
the Game

GRANTLAND RICE, *ONLY THE BRAVE*, 1855

Opposite: AUSTRALIA, above HOLLAND

SAUDI ARABIA

CHINA

CHINA

CHINA

AUSTRALIA

JAPAN

Opposite: ENGLAND, above: AUSTRALIA

Above and overleaf: AUSTRALIA

AUSTRALIA

Above, Sydney, Australia: keeping her head at Bondi Beach.

Page 61, Everberg, Belgium: dressing-room revelry for the junior soccer team,
a project supported by ICI.

Pages 62-63, Moshi, Tanzania: bathtime.

Page 64, Sydney, Australia: skate-boarding.

Page 65, top, Rotterdam, Holland: pavement-racing.
Bottom, Riyadh, Saudi Arabia: desert-karting.

Page 66, top and bottom, Shanghai, China: students of the Changning
Gymnastic School.

Page 67, top, Shanghai, China: students of the Changning Gymnastic School.
Bottom, New South Wales, Australia: limbering up at the Flying Fruit Fly
Circus School in Albury.

Pages 68-69, Tottori City, Japan:
17-year-old Yusaku Katagiri, the High School Sumo wrestling champion of
Japan, with colleagues from Jyohoku High School.

Page 70, London, England: sparring partners at Repton Boys' Club.

Page 71, top and bottom, New South Wales, Australia: pupils of the
Flying Fruit Fly Circus School in Albury.

Pages 72-73, Sydney, Australia: junior life-savers in training at
Maroubra Beach.

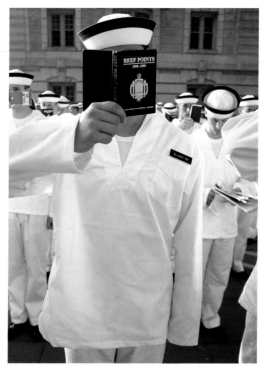

Above and overleaf: USA

*He who conquers
others is strong;
He who conquers himself
is mighty*

LAO-TZE, *THE CHARACTER OF TAO*, 6TH C. BC

SWITZERLAND

Above: PAKISTAN, opposite: CHINA

78

Opposite: SPAIN, above: AUSTRALIA

USA

Above, Maryland, USA: women at arms.
Female recruits at the United States Naval Academy in Annapolis follow
precisely the same routines as their male counterparts.

Pages 75-77, Maryland, USA:
plebes (new recruits) at the United States Naval Academy.

Page 78, top, Zurich, Switzerland: at the annual parade of the city's guilds.
Bottom, Karachi, Pakistan: morning assembly at a primary school.

Page 79, Shanghai, China: on the outskirts of the city, police close the road for
five minutes each morning so the pupils of the Zhejiang Road Primary School
can do their morning exercises.

Page 80, Vilafranca, Spain: 11-year-old Dori Vazquez Leiva tops this
human tower (castell).

Page 81, New South Wales, Australia: young acrobats in training at
the Flying Fruit Fly Circus School in Albury.

MALAYSIA

*M*an makes holy what he
believes as he makes beautiful
what he loves

ERNEST RENAN, 1857

Preceding pages: SPAIN, above: USA

Above: OMAN, opposite: INDIA

Above: OMAN, overleaf: INDONESIA

PAKISTAN

PAKISTAN

PAKISTAN

PAKISTAN

93

Above and preceding pages: JAPAN

JAPAN

PERU

Above, Cuzco, Peru:
posing for the family album after first communion in the Cathedral.

Page 83, Melaka, Malaysia: abandoned on the steps of a temple at birth,
two orphans embrace the Buddhist faith in return for a home.

Pages 84-85, Catalonia, Spain:
the choristers of Montserrat prepare for midday Salve.

Page 86, top, New York State, USA:
orthodox teenage Jews, Gan Israel summer camp.
Bottom, Muscat, Oman: studying the Koran at The Sultan's School.

Page 87, Calcutta, India: turbaned Sikhs at Khalsa English High School.

Pages 88-89, Salalah, Oman:
spectators in the women's stand, National Day celebrations.

Pages 90-91, Java, Indonesia: prayer time for teenage Muslim girls
at a religious school in Yogyakarta.

Pages 92-93, Karachi, Pakistan:
at a madrassa (religious school), boys study the Koran until they can
recite it word for word.

Pages 94-97, Kamakura, Japan: 18-year-old Yomey Hayashi, a novice monk,
performs his daily tasks at the Myo-Honji temple.

USA

*Where there is
no hope there can be
no endeavour*

SAMUEL JOHNSON, *THE RAMBLER*, 1750–1752

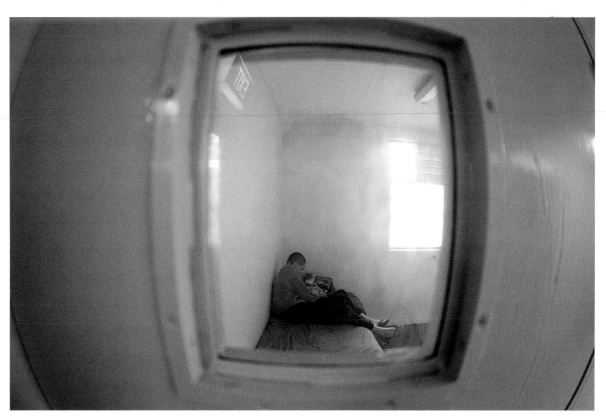

Opposite: ENGLAND, above: AUSTRALIA

INDONESIA

TANZANIA

Above and opposite: TANZANIA

Opposite and above: PERU

PERU

Preceding pages: TURKEY, above: BANGLADESH

Above and opposite: SOUTH AFRICA

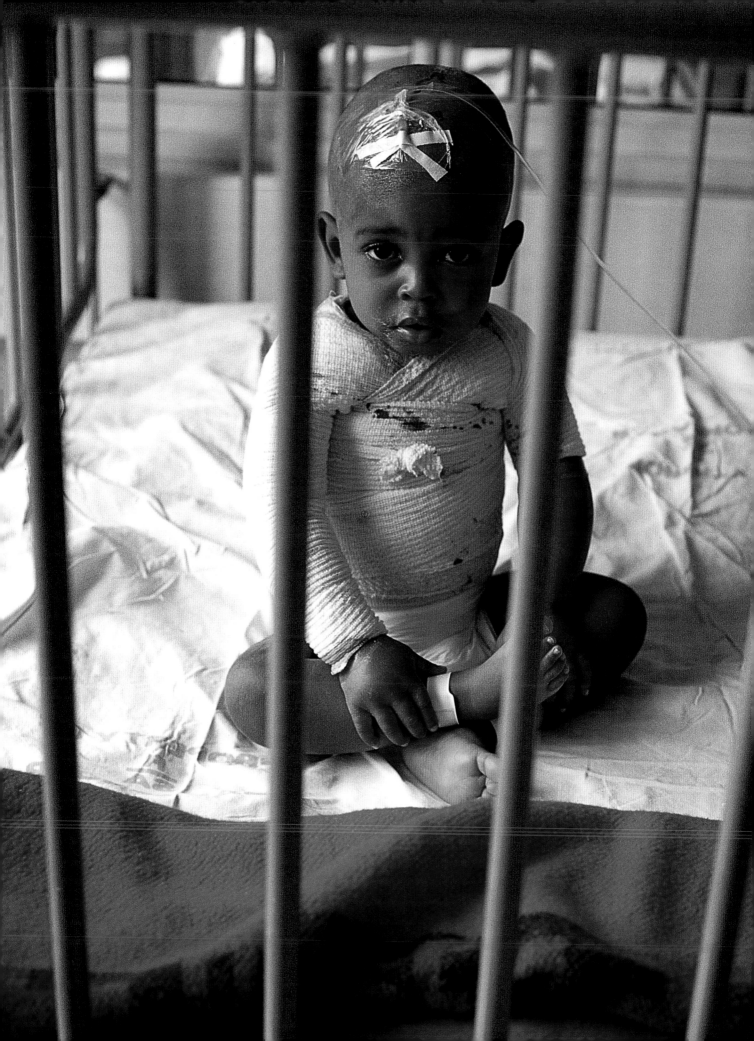

LUXEMBOURG

Above, Luxembourg: refugees from Kosovo find shelter at
a government centre.

Page 99, New York City, USA: demonstrating for her rights in Harlem.

Page 100, London, England: living rough and fighting drugs.

Page 101, top, Sydney, Australia: juvenile detention centre.
Bottom, Western Sumatra, Indonesia: on a Bukittinggi street.

Page 102, top, Moshi, Tanzania: living rough.
Bottom, and Page 103, Moshi, Tanzania: the Mkombozi Centre for Street
Children.

Pages 104-105, Lima, Peru: a residential centre for street children in Lima.
Prevention of drug abuse is the centre's prime concern. The teaching of trades
such as baking helps prepare the teenagers for life back in the community.

Pages 106-107, Ankara, Turkey: alone with the beating of her heart.

Page 108, top, Bangladesh: a provincial hospital.
Bottom, Soweto, South Africa: suffering from rickets, a child waits for an
operation at the Chris Hani Baragwanath hospital.

Page 109, Soweto, South Africa: the burns unit of the Chris Hani
Baragwanath hospital.

JAPAN

*M*usic and rhythm
find their way into the secret
places of the soul

PLATO

Previous spread: SOUTH AFRICA, above: LUXEMBOURG

Above: SPAIN, opposite: PAKISTAN

Opposite: SPAIN, above: CHINA

Above: ENGLAND, overleaf: INDIA

117

Opposite: SPAIN above: HUNGARY

USA

ENGLAND

Above, Richmond, England:
a pupil at the Royal Ballet School, White Lodge.

Page 111, Tokyo, Japan: Taiko drummers at the Nezu shrine.

Pages 112-113, Katlehong township, South Africa: pupils of Monde Primary
School in full voice.

Page 114, top, Luxembourg: The Luxembourg Conservatoire de Musique.
Bottom, Catalonia, Spain: at audition for the Choir School of Montserrat.

Page 115, Karachi, Pakistan:
music to paint by at the Indus Valley School of Art and Architecture,
a project supported by ICI Pakistan.

Page 116, Catalonia, Spain: playing traditional instruments, the young men of
Breda lead their gegants (giants) to the village festa.

Page 117, top, Shanghai, China: traditional instruments are also the choice of
these students at the Yanan Middle School.
Bottom, High Wycombe, England: impromptu performance at Godstowe
Preparatory School.

Pages 118-119, Kerala, India: Krishnattam, a dance-drama
performed at the Guruvayoor temple, relates the story of Krishna, played here
on the right by 14-year-old K.M. Maneesh, who joined the temple as
a trainee dancer at the age of eight.

Page 120, Granada, Spain: outside the Mariquilla Flamenco Dance Centre.

Page 121, top, Mikofalva, Hungary: teenage members of
the traditional folk dance group.
Bottom, Arizona, USA: competing at the annual Navajo powwow
at Window Rock.

Above: GERMANY, overleaf: SPAIN

*W*hat of soul was left, I wonder,
when the kissing had to stop?

ROBERT BROWNING

Opposite: SPAIN, above: ENGLAND

ENGLAND

ENGLAND

SPAIN

USA

USA

ENGLAND

Above, Henley-on-Thames, England: Henley Royal Regatta.

Page 123, Hamburg, Germany.

Pages 124-126, Ibiza, Spain: clubbing.

Page 127, top and bottom, Reading, England: the Reading Festival.

Page 128, top, Buckinghamshire, England: boys from Eton College meet the
girls from Wycombe Abbey School for their annual Caledonian Ball.
Bottom, Spain: British holiday-makers.

Page 129, top and bottom, Kansas, USA: in an attempt
to reduce the high rate of unwanted pregnancies amongst pupils,
demanding computerized dolls are used in sex education
programmes at North Kansas City High School, supported by
National Starch, an ICI subsidiary.
Pupils who already have babies can bring them into class.
A new crèche for these pupil parents will help ease their burden.

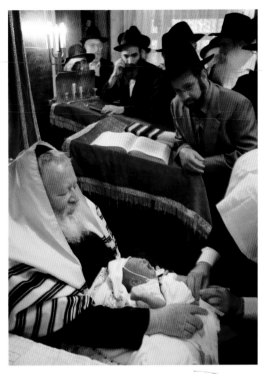

Above: USA, overleaf: PERU

*The four stages of man are
infancy, childhood, adolescence
and obsolescence*

ART LINKLETTER

TANZANIA

TANZANIA

Above: TANZANIA, overleaf SOUTH AFRICA

AUSTRALIA

AUSTRALIA

Above: AUSTRALIA, overleaf: ENGLAND

MOROCCO

Opposite and above: INDIA

JAPAN

Above and opposite: JAPAN

Opposite: INDONESIA, above: INDIA

CHINA

USA

Above, New York, USA: a young Jewish bride waits to join her
husband-to-be for the marriage ceremony in Brooklyn.

Page 131, New York, USA:
circumcision for a Rabbi's son at a synagogue in Brooklyn.

Pages 132-133, Cuzco, Peru: first communion for boys at the Cathedral.

Pages 134-135, Oldeani, Tanzania: wearing black as a sign of their recent
circumcision and progression into manhood, Masai teenagers leave their homes
to roam the bush and train as warriors.

Pages 136-137, Kwamabhoko, South Africa: keeping to the strict rules of
personal adornment, young circumcised Ndebele girls wear beaded hoops
around their legs to celebrate their initiation into womanhood.

Pages 138-139, Armidale, Australia:
the Summer Ball for debutantes and their partners.

Pages 140-141, Oxford, England:
graduates receive their degrees at the University of Oxford.

Page 142, Calcutta, India:
leavers celebrate their last day at Loreto House School.

Page 143, top, Atlas mountains, Morocco: marriageable young women of the
Ait Hadiddou Berber tribe gather nervously at Imilchil for the annual bridal fair.
Bottom, Calcutta, India: leavers at Loreto House School.

Pages 144-145, Tokyo, Japan: after the marriage ceremony, dressers
and beauticians prepare the bride for the official photographs at Meji Shrine.

Page 146, West Sumatra, Indonesia: bride and groom await their
guests at Batang Palupuh.

Page 147, top, Delhi, India: held aloft by wedding guests, a young
couple celebrate their wedding in a suburb.
Bottom, Hong Kong, China: friends check the bridal gown at the register office.

ACKNOWLEDGMENTS

I could not have produced the pictures for this book without the help and support of so many people, and I hope they especially will enjoy the results of our joint endeavours.

I particularly want to thank Claire Louise Bean for her help throughout the project.

Penelope Cream, Martin Jennings, Rosemary Luker, Sophie Raynor, Helen Thompson and Jane Williams all did invaluable research and vital long-distance planning.

My thanks to Jo Anderson for guiding me through Masai land, and to Maria Mbambela for introducing me to the Ndebele community outside Johannesburg.

I am enormously grateful to Jasmine Mu for opening so many doors in China, and to Junko Katano for doing the same in Japan. And, while Indonesia was tearing itself apart, Mie Cornoedus not only continued to dispense much-needed refreshments from her excellent cafe but became a fixer of extraordinary dexterity.

I am indebted to Ros Bible for managing my debut in Albury; to Jean, Juana and Nadine Feyder for their inspiration, guidance and hospitality; and to Emmanuelle Stefanidis for lending her support.

The head teachers, principals and directors of all the schools, colleges, academies and institutions who gave me free access to the young people in their care all have my heartfelt thanks, as do Professor Issy Segal and administrators of the Chris Hani Baragwanath Hospital in Soweto, and Pietie Sarink at the Sophia Children's Hospital in Rotterdam.

I am very grateful to the Lubavitch organization for the help they gave me in Brooklyn, and to the families there who welcomed a stranger and his cameras to their various celebrations. At the other end of New York in Harlem, Millie and Chris Rosario were generous with their time and with helpings of good food, and I thank them warmly for both.

And my special thanks to Ben and Susannah Lloyd-Shogbesen, who were warm and generous in letting me photograph their daughter-in-waiting.

Finally, Gillian Ashley was more than generous with her time in finding apposite words to introduce the pictures: my thanks to her. And without Joanna Dale's considerable editing and design skills, there would be no book, just a huge and loose collection of pictures.

Above: PAKISTAN, opposite: PERU

AUSTRALIA

Above, Australia: playtime at the Toomelah Aboriginal Mission school.

Page 1, London, England: spectators at the Notting Hill Carnival.

Page 3, Arizona, USA:
a visitor to the annual Navajo powwow at Window Rock.

Page 5, Selangor, Malaysia: dressed for the mosque.

Page 6: school leaders.

Pages 8-9, Tanzania: Masai children at play as the sun goes down.

Page 10, Kuala Lumpur, Malaysia: a secret shared.

Page 150, Karachi, Pakistan: boot ride.

Page 151, the Andes, Peru: mountain girl on the lower slopes.